This book is based on life experience, thoughts, feelings, dreams and wishes that have yet to come true! The world can be a beautiful place, but only *if* we make it that way. Life can get us down; our determination and perseverance can help us stand up again, and again, never quit! As much as we give and share, we deserve the returns. So, don't stop believing. It's our perception in life that makes us happy and at peace, and all of the above expressed in poetry comes from deep within me!

Life at its best—not what it could be, but what we need to see—inspired me to write. I dedicate this to my family and friends, who have always been by my side!

Therese Rodrigo

BEAUTIFUL IS THE LIFE…

AUSTIN MACAULEY PUBLISHERS
LONDON • CAMBRIDGE • NEW YORK • SHARJAH

Copyright Therese Rodrigo 2025

The right of Therese Rodrigo to be identified as author of this work has been asserted by the author in accordance with sections 77 and 78 of the Copyright, Designs and Patents Act 1988.

All rights reserved. No part of this publication may be reproduced, stored in a retrieval system, or transmitted in any form or by any means, electronic, mechanical, photocopying, recording, or otherwise, without the prior permission of the publishers.

Any person who commits any unauthorised act in relation to this publication may be liable to criminal prosecution and civil claims for damages.

A CIP catalogue record for this title is available from the British Library.

ISBN 9781035887392 (Paperback)
ISBN 9781035887408 (ePub e-book)

www.austinmacauley.com

First Published 2025
Austin Macauley Publishers Ltd®
1 Canada Square
Canary Wharf
London
E14 5AA

I would like to give a special thanks to my mother, who gave me the idea and motivation to do this book.

Also, I would like to thank everyone in my life who's taken me places through all the emotions and life experiences I have had that helped to express my thoughts in this book of poetry.

I would like to thank Hiruni Hansika for helping me with the images.

I take this opportunity to thank the team at Austin Macauley Publishers for the prompt responses, efficiency and support extended to me in handling the publication of the book.

Preface

My words in this book reflect my perception of this world and, in other words, what *if!* My feelings and thoughts revolve around the people in my life. Unspoken words of a young girl or a woman may be theirs and my emotions and dreams that hoped and hopes still to come true.

What I wish the world could be and how if it were, beautiful is the life for us to have and to hold. Although most often everything we plan doesn't go the way we want it to, be daring to leap over, cross that rocky road, and jump that hurdle. But believing and having hope is the light we go towards, and we shall go to that finish line of our set goals.

So, when our call comes, you know you've lived the life of your dreams. Pure and humble heart, which conquers this world not by fame and riches, but that of you enjoyed the beauty of the ground we walk on, in the simplest of ways; we have won it all!

Beautiful is the Life...

For us to make,
For us to keep.
Every day, make it happen,
Give and no return
Gratitude of any,
Is what we must, not expect in return.

Good things of all,
Share must you,
Give and give away,
To the one who needs most.

But don't be disheartened,
If return one does not,
Gratitude of any.
Because of what we do,
Because of what we give,
Is a story that we share,
With only the one above.

Do and be forgotten,
Of all the deeds that you do.
Blessings when they come,
Plenty in full,
Is yours to keep,
And to hold.

Beautiful is the life,
When you can share,
Delight and be joyful,
In giving and to part with,
what was yours to have.

When You Fall in Love

What is love so true?
That moment when you see
The spark and the chemistry
Blends in a potion of magic,
That ignites a fire inside,
And gives a connection,
Goose bumps and chills,
Like no other.

The thought of that love in your life
Makes you smile for no reason,
Makes you feel complete,
And you know,
Found you have,
That special someone it is
Sealed with love.

Strong as concrete,
Stuck like glue,
Is what it is,
When
Love is caring,
Love is giving,
Love is sharing,
Love is unconditional.
Appreciate and be appreciated,
Respect and be respected,
Understand to be understood.
When you see that's your soulmate,
Eyes that see are only yours.

Every beat of their heart,
Guarded by your love.
Addicted you get,
You just can't do without.
When that feeling you get
'I don't need anything else, but him or her.'

Where you just laugh at their jokes,
Feel free and talk about anything,
Tell them your desires,
Tell them the darkest secrets.
Judged, you will not be.

Feel free to cry,
Don't fear them, but feel safe,
Simplest of time spent together
Is what you cherish the most.

Then, no matter what the life storms are,
What bad weathers come your way,
Eternal mate are they,
And you shall never be apart,
As long as your soul is in your body,
And together till death do us part.

Is a *love* so true!

Deception

Deception it is,
All the beauty of love,
All the love devoted
Without batting an eyelid.
Faithfully surrendered
To the one you believe is yours,
Loyally loved… And yet
One gets betrayed
To all of the above.

Deception it is,
When trust is broken
By striving to do better
Better than you think;
What you have.

Deception…
Is it worth it?

All the simplest things we have
Are more of value,
That money cannot buy.
Live a honest life,
Than the fake appearances
That come before you,
That promises temporarily,
satisfaction of an infatuation,
…And you lose it all.

Life

Life is a blessing
Wherever it maybe
That we are born.

It's beautiful,
This thing called life,
If everything falls into place *but,*
Though maybe some days
Though, maybe sometimes,
Going into years,
But we have to make it,
Make life happen
No matter how rough the road gets;
Tougher the times
Challenges us most.

In life,
We all have a mission;
Mission untold,
Which we have to unfold.
Jump the hurdles,
Bear the pain,
Sacrifices made,
To make it to that place.

To some maybe,
Climb the ladder
Till you reach the top.
Find the money
To feed your own.
Find the soulmate
Your heart has longed.
Find the love
Of true and rare
Climb the highest point
Before you're called.

So, in life,
We are eternally,
Striving to make it,
to reach our goals,
rich or poor,
we work so hard
to get to the *top*
and shine like a star.

But, sometimes,
We work so hard
With great ambition,
And forget to mind that,
The simplest things
That surrounds us,
Neglected and forsaken.

In that moment of greatness,
With the spotlight on,
Being a star in the limelight,
Reached that victory,
And right to the top,
Stand alone, you do.

Forgetting the beginning
And the sacrifices made
By the ones around you,
And the race ran
To get to that place.

In that moment of loneliness
Everything falls apart,
Million pieces you're broken into,
As you are standing alone
And lost the most valuable,
Against the triumph.

This is life,
A balance must be,
Of your race to the top,
Then you hold in your hand,
The trophy of life,
Where everything falls in place,
And love you have
Treasured the most,
When you leave this world.

My Mother

You are a blessing,
A *blessing* for this world.
You strived to make it,
Make it in this world,
And you *made it!*
Made it to the best of the best.

Whilst striving to make it,
You became a miracle for others.
Making their dreams a reality.
Lived by example and in dignity.

Hard work joyfully done,
Laboured to the maximum,
An *order*, but always a helping hand;
Never say *no* to anyone in need!

There's a special place for you
In all of us,
There's a special place for you
Above!

Love always!

What a Friend He is

My Lord,
No words can describe
He's the star in my life.
Through the joys of my life,
You were
"Footprints in the sand",
And carried me in my pain.

My eternal friend, he shall be,
As there's no other,
Who couldn't be more loyal?
Listen to my woes,
Understand my cries,
Stand beside me, judgement made not.

He shows me the way
With opportunities given.
Spoken to me
in a language I'd understand,
through worldly signs
and circumstances,
that leads to the perfect answer
that my heart has longed.

You just have to listen,
And you shall hear.
Look, and you shall find.

He died for us,
To redeem us.

Yet we live to sin,
And multiple times.
From my first breath into this world,
Until I leave with my last,
The only loyal friendship,
Is what I have in Jesus.

My Dream

I have a dream,
A beautiful home,
Mansion it is not.
A love so true,
That's only for me.

To live in harmony,
Without animosity,
In perfect tranquillity,
With my brothers and sisters
All over the world.

Beautiful home,
That is warm in colour,
Home to be free,
Without rules and boundaries.
A view of a lake
Or waves rolling in,
Where I sit on a terrace,
Enjoy a cup of tea
As the sun rises,
Or a glass of wine
As the sun sets,
Over the horizon,
And thank God for every day
That I'm blessed to see.

A love so true,
Being my utmost desire,
Someone to hold,
Someone to love,
Someone who believes,
That you're their blessing.
Their eyes only see
The beauty of your love!
No matter how they look,
Beautiful or not.
Kindness is warm,
Respect is ineffable,
And all of the above,
Is yours to keep.

Tell me,
Where do I find this love so true?
So, I can place that soul,
Right inside my home
That's in my dream.

True Friend

Make a friend,
A friend so true,
It's a gift of life
That cannot be measured.

A friend so true;
Who stands by you,
In good and bad
is hardest to find.

Listen when you talk
A shoulder when you cry,
Smile when you're happy
Joyful at your success.
Faithfully and loyally
Stands by you,
When the world is against,
And you are alone.

Alone you shall not be
Because you have a friend,
Who is so true
Who'll never let you down,
 Rarest in this world
Is loyalty received,
But when you find that friend,
Treasure 'em for life.

Unruffled and Tranquil...

Calm and tranquil
Flow deep and shallow,
long and wide,
Runs through the forests
And mountains high.

Watch the water,
So tranquil
The gush of wind,
The crisp sound of leaves,
That blow over the river,
And that flow of the water,
Makes me feel,
So appease
Hush, and then listen.

While the nature itself
Harness and enjoy,
All of God's creatures,
Big and small,
Wild and tame,
Taste it all.

We must rejoice,
And must respect
And give its dues
Protect what's ours.

As the Waves Roll

Home of the beasts,
Under the water;
Deep and shallow,
Over the depths, are
Rolling waves.

At times, I think
When the waves hit hard
Against the giant rocks,
And the ocean is rough
That it's angry at us,
For we've done wrong.

But when I see
The sea so calm,
Soft waves splash
At the rocks around,
Into the night,
And clear skies,
When the moon reflects
On the calm sea water,
It's all breathtaking,
And that we're blessed to see.

While the creatures of the sea,
Enjoy it most
Whilst it's their home,
We must do it all
To keep their peace.

A Partner in Matrimony

Formal it sounds,
But that's what it is,
When we fall in love
Tie the knot, we do.

Have and to hold,
In good times and bad,
Sickness and health,
Till death us do part,
Vows that are made,
In this chapter of one's life.

It's a bond that is built,
In all good and bad.
Weddings and festive,
All celebrations may be,
Is a way past it all,
When reality hits
And you must face it all.

A love so strong,
Faithful and loyal,
Chemistry untold,
Shall withstand that's tough,
And hold it together,
This matrimonial bond.

Nothing and nobody
Could set apart,
A love that's so strong.
Though on paper
It may be,
What holds it together
Is the flame that's eternal,
Keeps burning in your heart.

Know if you must,
When we take up this life,
Of matrimonial bliss,

Be true to your heart,
Partner you must love,
With all due respect,
Devotion that's boundless.

A Proud Mother

To be blessed I am,
With the seeds of life
That grew in me,
Is the biggest miracle,
The greatest gift,
The Lord has given to me.

My two sons,
The greatest men
They've grown to be,
Great but humble,
Full of love,
And a gentleman
Both grown up to be.

They are my life
My greatest joy,
My accomplishment,
Is how I feel,
That brings me pride
In what they've learnt,
Values instilled
They still believe.

All the time we spent
In the simplest ways,
Chats we had,
Bedtime stories
And Marvel movies!

Travelled the world,
Saw the most,
And fun we had
Are memories now,
That I cherish the most.

'What's the menu?'
Is the frequent question,
Always ahead
Of a day or two,
Eating food.

That I kept making,
Critiques were they
That kept me going.
To do more and more
Just to see that smile
And then tell me,
"Mum, this is really good"
Makes me smile and then make more!

My two boys,
I love you more
Than you'd ever know.

When I'm gone
I'll tell the angels,
Please *keep* walking by their side,
Was my always constant prayer,
And forever shall be!

To be Like a Child

The heart of a child
Is pure and clean.
Written on their face
Innocence untold.

Speak their mind
And voice their heart,
How they feel
And what they are.

Mean no harm
And gives no pain,
Love is longed,
And shared the same.

What they want most,
Is to be like a child,
Play like a child
Is what they long.

Don't take that away
From that age
Of pure innocence
And childish ways.

Cos soon enough
They'll grow up
And miss that time
They should have had.
It's what we do
And how we treat them
That a child becomes
Who they are.
What we instil
In their innocent minds,
And play with them
In their content world.

It comes from above,
When the Lord said,
'Easily no two words,
Kingdom you shall enter,
Bear you must,
A heart of a child!'

As long as we
Guide their way
And help them
To be on their way
To the life that awaits,
Is the best we can do.

A Broken Heart

To love someone,
To be loved
In a bond unbroken
Is how it starts.

Romantic walks,
Holding hands,
Unstoppable,
The warm embraces,
Cuddles and kisses,
Are endless affections,
Romance is when it starts.

Feel like "walking on cloud nine",
Smile for no reason
Because the thought of them,
Makes life complete,
And your body reacts
In goose bumps and chills
That makes you happy
In a way that never did before.

Somewhere down
The road of life,
Temptations and all bad things
Get in the way,
And that bond gets broken
With betrayal.
As your world
Crumbles around you
And you feel like you can't breathe,
All of a sudden,
Into million pieces,
A heart gets broken.
That destroys you
From within an explosion;
All you want to do
Is roll up and die.

That cuts like a knife
Right through your heart.
Not the same feel as
When cupid struck!

Please don't break
This patched-up heart,
As it has been to,
Hell and back.

Don't want this burning pain,
A dream that seemed hopeless,
Can't take this any more
A broken heart no more!

Stand by Me

Stand by me
When I'm good,
Stand by me
When I'm not.

Hold me tight
With your warm caress,
Don't let go
Keep me loved and safe.

Raise me up
When I fall down,
Stand by me,
When the world is not.

Walk with me
'Cos I've lost my way,
Please take that time,
And spend it with me.

Give me strength
'Cos mine is weak,
Hold me close
When we lay down.

I need kind,
I need love,
I need warm;
Your sweet embrace!

She

She's somebody's mother
Who works so hard,
Sacrifices made
To be the light,
And be the strength,
And keep the smile,
And say, 'All's going to be okay.'
Even when it's not,
To her always; her baby!

She's somebody's daughter,
Loves them for all, and
For being blessed with life.
Will care and do,
All in her might
To see them through.
Until the calling
Heaven knows when.

She's somebody's woman;
Loves him with all her heart,
Faithfully in abundance,
Will walk that walk,
And take that hurt
And cry that tear,
Silently, and he knows not.

He does not know
What he holds,
Is so much worth
Than all the wealth
In this "so fake" world.

She's somebody's friend,
Shoulder to cry on,
Laugh when you laugh,
And embrace in joys.
Jealous she is not
when you reach the top
Because she's true,
Proud of her sis

She's a survivor!

When I Love

My love is pure,
Deeper than the ocean,
Stronger than you think.
Steadfast and passionate;
Longer than a river.

When I fall in love,
I love completely.
I give my all
And he becomes my everything.
The air that I breathe
Wind beneath my wings
Smile on my face,
Every beat of my heart.

When I love,
I'm a slave to his soul
He'll keep me on my toes,
Forever make him happy,
Promises never broken
That's who I am
That's what I do
When I fall in love.

The euphoria
I find in loving him,
Fulfilling my desires, a love that's endless,
Is his to have.

Fear

Fear is a weakness
Fear is unstoppable
When it gets instilled
In the mind of the conscious.

Fear is not alone
Of physical reactions,
It goes deep
As to words that are spoken.
When the world makes you feel
You're not good enough.

Fear is hurting,
And lonely in a world where
There is no respect.
Tainted with fear
Is not the greatest
Of emotions to hold.

Fear is a reason to
Hold your head up high,
Pretend to the world
Everything is all right.

Fight that fear
Stand up for you,
You know that you deserve
A whole lot more,
And good things in life.

Fight that battle,
Believe in yourself,
Stand up for your rights.
Step on that fear
And crush it to death,
'Cos you are stronger
More than you think,
To outlive this fear,
That shadows on our path.

Someone

Someone to love,
Someone to care,
Someone to understand and
Stand by your side.

Hugs and kisses,
Cuddles and warmth,
Gentle embraces.
Hand in hand,
Strolls in the park,
Picnics and fun times.

Candle-lit dinners,
Sun sets and moonlight,
Eyes only for you,
Sees only you,
And loves only you.

Faithfully and loyally,
Yours to be always,
Until one day
Good Lord calls,
And we go our own way.

Father

The love of a father
Is calm and quiet,
He speaks not,
He does what he has to;
A provider he is.

He cares with all,
But shares of it none.
The most that I find,
Is that he guards with his life,
What is his, he holds.

In the rush of this life,
Sometimes he forgets
Proud can he be,
Emotions to share,
Spoken or done.

I still reminisce
My father,
Man of few words
But actions were full;
How he demonstrated
His way of love.

My last dance
On my wedding day,
He held me so tight,
Controlled his tears,
And let me go,
As he knew then,
It was time for me
To leave the nest!
I'll always remember,
I'll always cherish,
The last moments I had,
Before he said goodbye
Took his last breath.

My Husband

Man of honour
He is,
Kind-hearted
And giving
Is all that he would do.

Provider to us all,
Care and loving,
A heart of gold
Is what he bears.

Duties of a man,
Husband and a father,
Son and a brother,
A friend and a good one,
Is what he is.

Blessings of plenty,
Is what I wish,
That he should have
And great success,
To the life that he holds.

God bless him always.

Italia

'Mi amore Italia!'
Is all that I can say,
Beautiful is a country
That I call my second home,
'Cos that's what I feel,
Every time I am in Italy.

Beautiful churches
That I can get lost all day in.
Tall marble pillars,
High sculptured ceilings.
Scenic paintings,
Sound of the organ music
That echoes through the church,
Makes you feel
That you're in heaven.
Sit and talk to God,
I thank him every time,
That I'm blessed to be here
In his house of many.

Besides all the churches,
The food I enjoy a lot,
A Gastronome I am
'Cos that's my passion.
Delicious food,
Different in each region,
Many a glass of wine,
And celebrations
Are quite the customary
In the hearts of all Italians,
Life they enjoy
Abundance in plenty.
Places of history,
Small narrow streets,
Lakes and fountains,
Romantic places,
Friendly people and each region
Has their special ways.
Fashion at its best,
Shopping to do plenty of,
Hobby that's my favourite!

Every time I walk into a place,
Greeted with a good day
Saying, 'Buongiorno'
Is quite welcoming
That I love the most.

La vita bella, in Italia!

Spoken with Flowers

Roses smell love,
Fresh, sharp and sweet!
Red, pink and yellow
Pure as white can be.

Many a shade and
Different colours
Of tulips and others.
Jasmine and lavender,
Lilies and orchids,
Bloom in different seasons,
Endless counts of flowers
This world has to offer.

Yellow is my favourite
Of roses that I love,
White lilies and jasmine,
purest and chaste.

An expression or a gesture,
Words unspoken,
An apology or two
A grateful thank you,
Is what we do with the above;
Of all of the flowers
That bloom in God's world.

How beautiful it would be.
This world could be,
As beautiful as the flowers,
An expression left forever.

Memories

Is what we have,
Childhood and growing up,
Early in our youth
And good times to hold.

Looking at pictures,
And smiling to ourselves,
Of the things we've done
That were forbidden!
But loved every minute,
Cherish them now,
Forever to keep.

We all have memories,
Good and the bad.
Lessons we have learnt,
In the midst of it all.
Dos and the don'ts,
But we've come out strong,
Still look back to then,
And love those recollections,
Of the good times we had
And bad we have learnt.

Memories we have,
Of our treasured families,
Those who are gone,
And the ones still remain.

Friends we have had,
Friends who still remain.
They play a special part,
In the lives that we have lived.
The times that we've shared,
Are great memories to hold,
As they'll never come around,
Like the way it did before.

Treasure them all,
And reminisce them all,
'Cos that is precious,
Lonely when we get,
To bring back a smile
Or laugh a laugh
That makes us happy
In the memories we hold.

I Love my Life

Thank you, my Lord,
Praise to the universe,
Thank you to this world
For this life that I have.

Every day when I wake up.
I give praise to my breath
That I have a roof over my head,
Strength in my body,
Joy in my heart.

As the sun rises
Over the horizon,
A beauty beyond compare
This world has to offer,
Yet not many see this,
The simplest of pleasures
Are so free at our reach.

I thank you again,
For all my blessings,
Little miracles,
We do not see.

Open our eyes wide,
Listen to the silence,
A small deed that's made
By someone you know.
Escape a misfortune,
That could have been you,
Missed by a minute or two.
That you're alive
And you're safe,
Are miracles of many
It's not hard to see.

But yet we lean on
What's not there
And yet to be.

Look to the sky so blue,
Rain, when it does,
Enjoy it the most.
Watch the sun rise,

Listen to the birds,
Sing in their glory,
To welcome each day.
Look at the beauty,
As the big orange sun,
Sets in the evening.

With all your might,
Be thankful for you,
Look and you'll see,
Listen and you'll hear,
Don't miss the chance
When opportunity knocks,
Miracles are waiting to,
Happen just for you.

Smile and a Laugh

What a smile can do
To make someone's day
Is a gift that is large,
Free as it can be,
Yours to be shared.

Smile, and smile again,
What it can do,
To someone who's low,
Drowned in sadness,
Lonely as can be,
Rejects of society,
Ignored and un-minded,
Of a simple acknowledgement
Of their existence.
A gesture of a little kindness
That goes a long way,
Through a simple smile
That gives it all!

The smile you can give,
That make them feel,
Somebody cares,
And somebody sees,
Who they are,
Become what they can.

That's why I say,
Smile away,
And make someone's day.

Laugh to your heart's content
Is good for your soul
And good for the spirit,
That's within you,
Needed a release of the
Tension on hold.

The best medicine they say,
Is a whole lot of laughter
Blended with a smile,
Becomes a cocktail of joy!

Smile when you can,
You make the world smile.
Laugh and laugh away,
Enjoy this life.

Be happy and do share,
The joy that you find,
Is the greatest gift,
To the world you can offer.

Wars of our Time

Why do we fight
To hold what's not,
Ours to keep?

From the start of time,
Up to the present,
Constantly we are
In war and disputes,
Of a land that we've been given,
To live and enjoy
Is a lease while we last!

We live life like,
Rule the world we think,
But little do they know
We all have to go,
And leave it all behind.

Why can't we all have
Harmony and live
With the life that we're blessed?
Fight we must not,
For the boundaries set.

Sacrificed lives,
Of many and too much,
Poor are the most,
Hardest that's hit.
Children are many,
Don't get to see,
What life has to offer.
Poor they become,
And orphaned too,
Solitude is theirs,
Lonely and lost.

What greed can do,
Is a sad situation,
Hunger for the power,
Fame and fortune,
Brings to an end,
Of a world than can be,
A paradise to live.

Bonded by Blood

Bonded by blood,
Is stronger than any,
My love for my brother,
Is true to the last word.
A bully he can be,
But I love my big brother,
No matter what he does!

When the days that we were,
Young and carefree,
Fight and make up
Was a part of that life.

Beautiful childhood bliss
Are the days that I miss.

As time passed us by
We found our own lives,
Avenues that are different
And families to be with.

I still remember,
The times that we had,
Playing house and having fun,
And pranks that we pulled!
Carolling during Christmas
Fun times we had.
An early morning wake-up,
To pick the olives that dropped
From our grandmother's garden.
Innocence at its best,
Were the days of old.

But still, he would be
A brother to me,
Amidst the chaos
Of this godforsaken world.

Forgive and Forget Not

Forgive someone
Is the hardest to do,
When they've done wrong,
Hurt and the pain,
All the betrayal,
Of the trust that was placed,
Pardon that deed
That left scars untold.

Heart that was broken,
Million pieces to bind,
Pick up the pieces,
Patch up the heart,
Move on to the next,
Chapter of life.
Beginning of new,
Hopes alive!

Sorry can be,
Things that don't matter,
Little deeds can let go,
For the smallest errors,
Rectified and settled,
In harmony so sweet.

Matters of the heart,
Bonds that are broken,
Betrayal at large,
Difficult are they,
To forgive and be forgotten.

As they carry in their soul,
The hurt and the pain,
Pushed back may be,
Never to be spoken.

Circumstances are a few,
A flashback that happens,
Of a memory that's pushed back,
Comes into the light.
Reminder, it does,

Of the pain and tears,
It's like poking a wound,
That's never really healed,
Of the forgiven but not forgotten.

Forgive we must,
Forget is hard,
Forgive and to forget
If it can be done,
Is the greatest gift to
Have and to hold!

All Material Things

Beautiful it is,
We have things and own,
Call it our mansion,
Many we have are possessions.
Houses and villas,
Beautifully decorated,
Some might own one,
And others own many.

Cars that are fancy,
Definitely more than
One for the week,
Another for the weekend.

Some would be born with it,
Others grow to own it.
While some others destroy unity,
Of a beautiful partnership,
To get to that place,
And claim ownership.

One way or the other,
Worldly possession are they,
Called when its time
That we have to go,
Leave behind is what
We enjoyed while we had.
So,
Attached you must not be,
To all that is here,
All material things,
We have to leave behind.

Live must you, your life,
Carefree and happy,
Clear in your mind,
Love with all your heart.
Every moment of the day,
Give praise to be alive.

Harm you must not,
Even by a thought.
Give what you can,
Count not how much,
Let that be forgotten,
A good deed,
It indeed would be.

Don't you Quit

Don't quit,
You must not.
Hardest when hit,
Tallest you stand.

We all have a mission,
To run the race,
Work hard must we,
Goals we must claim.

Life hits you hard,
When delays there are,
The road looks rocky,
Stormy days can be there,
Times get tougher,
And the climb seems steep,
But quit you must not.

You will get there,
Work hard and work around it,
There's always a way,
Positive must you think,
Believe in yourself,
It's just at your reach,
You just have to get there.

Don't you quit!

Universe

It's beautiful and everything,
Is what the universe can be.
We are just another planet,
Among the others,
In its existence
Among the billions of stars,
And mysteries yet to unfold.

Stars they shine
Fall to the earth sometimes,
Beautiful in the night.
Moon that we see,
Half or a full,
Is a beauty of its own.

When the morning comes,
Sun rises to shine,
Another source of energy,
A star from the galaxy.
Ever so bright,
The earth gets graced by the birds,
And welcomes the day.
To help with our food,
And to help the earth grow.

Why we must destroy,
What is ours to live,
Preserve for the young,
Give them their turn,
Because we have lived ours.

Seasons so Beautiful

Beautiful are they,
Spring and the summer,
Autumn and the winter,
Cold and the snow,
Sunshine and rain.

Favourite of mine,
Is winter and the spring,
The cold and the frost,
In the midst of Christmas.
A change of season,
Spring it becomes,
Rays of sunshine,
To bloom the flowers.

Love the countries of seasons,
Which I enjoy the most.
Change my attire,
Being cozy and warm,
To
Tank tops and shorts.

Lovely it is,
We're blessed with the seasons,
Of different berries,
And seasonal food
Enjoyed the most!

Christmas

My favourite time of the year,
Tree that is the tallest,
In the home to display,
With tiny adornments,
Of the past and the new.

A month ahead.
Dried fruits that are cut,
Soaked in juices
Preserve it must be,
For number of days.
Before it goes into the oven
And a cake is baked,
Then laid to rest.

House be decorated,
With pine and Poinsettia,
And holly that's jolly.
Is what it is,
The feeling of Christmas
Now comes alive.

Brings out the crib,
Display of the family,
Sweet little Jesus was laid,
Was born in a stable.
Is of most importance,
Reasons of celebrations,
Of this special season,
Is birth of our Christ,
Must not be forgotten.

Angel lights and sparkles,
Fill the gardens,
And trees in the houses.

The smell of roast turkey,
Gravy to go with.
Baked herb potatoes,
And all other foods.
Eggnog and Christmas pudding,
Topped with brandy sauce,
Is the yummiest to have!

Then comes eve of Christmas,
Midnight mass
And warm wishes,
Exchanging of gifts,
Re-united with families,
Is the best kind of feeling,
That we all celebrate.

Loyal Fury Friend

Never will you find
faithful always be
Love that's huge to share
Is the fury friend we have.

Never will they measure,
The love they can offer.
As the loyalty lies,
With the one that took them in.
Gave them a home,
Gratitude at large,
Is what they've got to offer.

Welcome that's welcoming,
When you reach home,
Abundance of love
Is yours to have.

You will never find another,
As faithful and true,
Loyal and kind,
And a love that's enormous
Is theirs to give.

A Kind Heart

Think thoughts
That are pure and innocent.
Think thoughts
That are true to your heart.

Be kind and caring,
Thoughts of evil,
Should not be holding,
Forgive and forgotten.

Carefree and happy,
Each day we should live.
Good you must see,
In all people,
As the beauty you shall find is
"In the eye of the beholder".

Be happy and content,
In the smallest of pleasures.
Enjoy this life,
And the fruits of this world.
We've got one life,
Let's make the most,
Like there's no tomorrow.

Every beat of your heart,
May it be a symbol,
Of love, compassion and kind!

When you Know you Found Love

Beautiful are they,
Search no more,
I've found what I want,
In the depth of your eyes.

Fallen star it is,
That you are to me.
Where we meet,
As the river meets the ocean,
So the tide meets the stream,
Connected with the flow,
And can never be separated
Endless love that was meant to be.

In your arms,
Is my home,
And I feel safe,
Is what you are to me.

Unconditional is the love,
That I feel from you,
Is what I have for you,
That's when you know
You've found love.

Grand Sweet Mother

She is no more,
But sweet was her ways,
And devoted to us.

Little things she did,
Spoilt us every time,
Even when there was a don't!

Always made me feel,
Like I am the "queen" in her life!
Called me that too,
And made me feel loved.

Told us the stories,
Of fairytales plenty.
That grew in me,
Still living that fairytale dream!

Made sure to be there,
Every birthday was a must.
Birth of my children,
Her presence was the first.

Thereafter, to be there,
Celebrations of many,
Mine and her great children, too.

Glad that we got to see her,
Hear the stories,
That were wild and sweet,
Of my grandfather too, and
Of their tales and their times.

Our visits to her home,
Was an event in her life
She treasured most.
With the simplest food,
Made with a spoonful
Of love.

Looking back, now I feel,
Best days of my childhood life,
Were the times spent,
Another dimension of time
Free from automation,
When eyes meet actually,
Where life was just simple and carefree.

I thank my grandma always,
For the values instilled in me,
Is passed off to another generation
Of her great grandchildren too!

You Held me up

You raised me up
So I stand tall,
Against this world
Of the good and the ugly.

You held me up,
When I'm down
And broken.

You showed the way,
Rocky the road was.
Stormy seas I walked on
And you stood beside me.

You showed me how,
More than I can be.
I look back,
Proud I am,
Of the person I have become.

In spite of it all,
I stand tall,
And humble shall be.
I look up and say to you,
Thank you for all that I am.

Alone I did not walk,
You by my side,
I made it, and I love you.

The Last Chapter

This I want to be,
The best of all that was,
Dreams that were meant to be
Come true at last!

Rewrite the stars,
Would I, if I could have,
I'd have my way,
live the dream
Oh! Sweet dream indeed.

Tick the bucket list,
Pyramids must I see,
Safaris in the wild,
In the land of Africa.
Land of the holy,
I must go to.
Wide coastlines,
And places of many,
That I have to see.

When all that's done and finished,
Then I settle down to,
A place of peace and tranquil,
A life that's only mine,
And mine to be delighted,
It's free and uncomplicated.

Share the love I hold,
And be reciprocated
Is beautiful indeed.
Give your love with all,
Wholehearted, and plenty.

How great it would be,
Live in your place of fantasy,
Calm, lake and trees,
A sunrise or sun set,
Is a definite bliss!

Pray, that I do,
With all my heart it is,
Step into the dream I hold,
Make it come true for me,
Would be a beautiful ending,
To the final chapter of me.

Remember Me

Remember me
When I'm gone,
My thoughts I leave behind.

Enjoy life you must,
One life there is to have.
Do good and do no wrong.
Be kind and gentle,
To the heart that's needed most.

Be happy and joyful.
Fruits of this world
You must enjoy
'Cos we spend too much time,
Working too hard, it is,
Before you know it's time,
That we've missed the wonders,
Or the windows of opportunity,
We couldn't see through.

Grown too old.
We have indeed.
To see the splendours,
Of what the world has to offer.

All things that I did,
In all in good intention,
Greatest pleasure was mine!
Remember this always,
Give and don't speak,
Love and love passionately.
Loyal you must be,
Partner or a friend,
Respect is imperative,
It's a sign of a bond
that is the strongest

Whatever you do,
Forget you must not,
Smile and smile again,
You'd have made someone's day,
Is a gift that goes beyond,
No money can buy.

Be humble, simple, love, and give your all.
Returns are boundless for you to enjoy, in this thing called life!

Remember me

Remember me
When I'm gone,
My thoughts I leave behind.

Enjoy life you must,
One life there is to have.
Do good and do no wrong,
Be kind and gentle,
To the heart that's needed most.